The Anointing to Live: Accessing the Power - Avoiding the Pitfalls

Creflo A. Dollar Jr.

Unless otherwise indicated, all scripture quotations are taken from the King James Version of the Bible.

The Anointing to Live: Accessing the Power–Avoiding the Pitfalls
ISBN 1-885072-10-4
Copyright © 1997 by Creflo A. Dollar Jr.
World Changers Church International
P.O. Box 490124
College Park, GA 30349

Published by CREFLO DOLLAR PUBLICATIONS
P.O. Box 490124
College Park, GA 30349

Printed in the United States of America

CONTENTS

INTRODUCTION

How God anointed Jesus of Nazareth with the Holy Ghost and with power: who went about doing good, and healing all that were oppressed of the devil; for God was with him. (Acts 10:38)

It would be easy to think that everything one could possibly say about the anointing of the Holy Ghost has already been said. Countless books have been written about it. Untold sermons have explored the topic. And, especially in recent years, fresh revelation from mighty men and women of God has come forth on the anointing.

The fact of the matter is, however, the subject of the anointing is as deep and inexhaustible as the power of God itself.

A few years back I wrote a book about the anointing which incorporated most of what I knew about the subject at the time. It was called *Understanding God's Purpose for the Anointing.* Looking back, I realized I only scratched the surface with that book.

There is so much more we haven't begun to apply to our lives. So much we don't understand. And if we, the body of Christ, are to get where we need to be in these last days, we must have a greater understanding of how to live in the anointing and how the anointing enables us to live.

The End of Yokes and Burdens

In the fourth chapter of Luke, we find one of the most remarkable and important passages in all of scripture:

And he [Jesus] came to Nazareth, where he had been brought up: and, as his custom was, he went into the synagogue on the sabbath day, and stood up for to read. And there was delivered unto him the book of the prophet

1

[Isaiah]. And when he had opened the book, he found the place where it was written, "The Spirit of the Lord is upon me, because he hath anointed me to preach the gospel to the poor; he hath sent me to heal the brokenhearted, to preach deliverance to the captives, and recovering of sight to the blind, to set at liberty them that are bruised, to preach the acceptable year of the Lord." **(Luke 4:16-19)**

Why are these verses so important? Because, in them, Jesus states His mission and identifies Himself as the Anointed One prophesied in scripture. The one whose anointing will remove the burdens and destroy the yokes.

When Jesus sat down in the synagogue and read the above passage from Isaiah 61, He was declaring to all the world that He was "anointed." He declared that the anointing meant good news for poor people, healing for the sick or broken-hearted, plus deliverance and freedom for anyone oppressed or captive in any way.

After reading that passage he sat down and made what, for his Jewish listeners, was an earth-shaking statement:

...This day is this scripture fulfilled in your ears. **(Luke 4:21)**

Just a few weeks earlier Jesus had been baptized by John in the Jordan River. At the moment of His baptism, the Spirit of God descended like a dove "anointing" Him with the power of the Holy Ghost without measure.

This anointing was the same one the prophet Isaiah foresaw:

And it shall come to pass in that day, that his [Satan's] burden shall be taken away from off thy shoulder, and his yoke from off thy neck, <u>and the yoke shall be destroyed because of the anointing</u>. **(Isaiah 10:27)**

The anointing of Holy Ghost power that rested upon Jesus is the power to remove burdens and destroy yokes.

The terms "burden" and "yoke" are words that relate to beasts of burden. They refer to images of oxen in heavy wooden yokes pulling heavy loads, and donkeys trudging along with backs piled high.

This is precisely how most of the world lives. Satan is described in the Bible as "the god of this world" and those who live under his domain live life shackled by yokes of bondage such as addiction and fear. They labor under crushing loads of sickness, lack and relational strife.

The anointing Jesus announced comes to remove those burdens and destroy those yokes. In fact, the Hebrew word translated "destroy" means to progressively corrode until something is reduced to powder. The anointing doesn't just break yokes — it disintegrates them.

Learning to live in the freedom, joy and power the anointing provides is what this book is all about.

CHAPTER 1

THE COMING OF ANTICHRISTS

And it shall come to pass in that day, that his burden shall be taken away from off thy shoulder, and his yoke from off thy neck, and the yoke shall be destroyed because of the anointing. (Isaiah 10:27)

"The anointing destroys the yoke." This phrase has become a familiar one in many Christian circles. I've personally done a lot of teaching over the last few years about "the burden-removing, yoke-destroying power of the anointing."

That teaching has centered on the truth that the term *Christ,* literally translated, means "the Anointed One and His anointing."

In other words, the power of the Holy Spirit which rested in and upon Jesus is now available to us because we are "in Christ." (2 Corinthians 1:21; 5:17)

So, what does the anointing do? It removes burdens and destroys yokes. Are there any burdens the anointing cannot remove? Any yokes it cannot destroy? No. The anointing of God is the most powerful force in the universe. There is nothing in this world or in Satan's domain that can withstand it.

There is, however, a force at work in the earth with the specific purpose of trying to stop the anointing from operating in your life. It is an anti-anointing force.

Now, keep in mind that the biblical word for the anointed one and His anointing is Christ. So what do you think the Bible calls this force that sets itself against the anointing? *Antichrist,* of course.

The Anti-Anointing

When most of us hear the term "antichrist," we immediately think of end-time prophecy and the evil person the book of Revelation calls "the beast." While this term certainly does apply to the individual mentioned in prophecy, the term antichrist has a broader meaning.

Look at 1 John 2:18, and you'll see what I mean:

Little children, it is the last time: and as ye have heard that antichrist shall come, even now are there many antichrists; whereby we know that it is the last time.

According to John, there were already many "antichrists" present in the earth in his day. By that we know he certainly couldn't have been referring to the beast of revelation.

He was talking about those people, things and evil spirits that are *against* the anointing. The name *antichrist* literally means "anti-anointed one and his anointing."

Anything in your life which tends to quench or hinder the anointing of God is an antichrist to you. That thing is anti-anointing.

Unforgiveness is anti-anointing. Bitterness, lying and gossip are anti-anointings. So are lust, slothfulness and lasciviousness. Anything that goes against the anointing has an antichrist or anti-anointing aspect to it.

Satan and his demonic spirits are not only out to keep you from operating in the anointing, but they also bring a form of anointing — a supernatural empowerment acting on human flesh-themselves.

Take, for example, the account of the "madman of Gadara" found in Mark, chapter five. There we see a supernatural demonic power working in the flesh of a man.

And when he was come out of the ship, immediately there met him out of the tombs a man with an unclean spirit, who had his dwelling among the tombs; and no man could bind him, no, not with chains: because that he had been often bound with fetters and chains, and the chains had

6

been plucked asunder by him, and the fetters broken in pieces: neither could any man tame him. (Mark 5:2-4)

What was the source of this man's supernatural strength? A destructive anointing from the anti-anointed one.

The Anointing in the Last Days

Notice the verse in 1 John concerning antichrists talked about knowing we're in the last days. He said, "...even now are there many antichrists; whereby we know that it is the last time."

Child of God, in these last days the anointing is the subject of the hour. Success, in these last days, is rapidly becoming a question of who is willing to pay the price and do the things to keep the anointing working in their lives.

Failure for believers will simply come down to the question of who allows the anti-anointing to quench the anointing in them.

The attacks of the devil you experience today are all about stopping the anointing. If he can get you to be offended, jealous, fearful or worried, he knows the level of anointing in you will diminish. And, Satan fears that anointing more than anything.

When the enemy comes up against a believer full of the anointing of God, he knows he doesn't stand a chance. That's why all of hell is focused on keeping you from doing the things that stir up the anointing, and to get you to do the things that quench it.

An Unction to Function

Immediately after warning his readers about the antichrists that are in the world trying to hinder their anointing, John went on to say something very interesting. Look at the next two verses:

They went out from us, but they were not of us; for if they had been of us, they would no doubt have continued with us: but they went out, that they might be made manifest that they were not all of us. But ye have an unction from the Holy One, and ye know all things. (1 John 2:19-20)

7

You "have an unction" from God. Did you know that? The word unction is an anointing word. It comes from a Greek word that means to smear or anoint with an ointment.

What is the purpose of this "unction" John is talking about? It is an unction that enables you to "know all things" that you need to know in order to get the job done. In other words, it's an unction to function.

Notice this doesn't say there's an anointing just to help preachers get the job done. It's not just for people in full-time ministry. No, this anointing is available to every believer.

It's available to parents to help them know how to raise their children. It's available to people in business to help them make wise business decisions and create "witty inventions."

In every job description and role in life, you have an unction, or anointing inside you that enables you to function supernaturally.

Whatever it is you do, God is saying, "I'm interested in you winning so, here's an anointing to help you do it."

You can tap into the anointing anytime you want. It's there for you to know the things you need to know, just when you need to know them.

Of course, no one in the natural can know all things. But, with the unction to function, you have an anointing to draw on knowledge and wisdom from God whenever you need it. In another part of scripture this is called "having the mind of Christ." (1 Corinthians 2:16)

Be a Know-It-All

A few verses later John gives us a key to understanding what this anointing we've been talking about is for. Look at 1 John 2:25:

And this is the promise that he hath promised us, even eternal life.

The word translated "life" in that verse is the Greek word zoe. It means "the God-kind of life." It's the abundant, victorious life you can experience right here in this world when the anointing of God is on you and in you. This unction to function is the anointing to live!

In the following verses we see once more how this unction brings you supernatural understanding and knowledge to win:

These things have I written unto you concerning them that seduce you. But the anointing which ye have received of him abideth in you, and ye need not that any man teach you: but as the same anointing teacheth you of all things, and is truth, and is no lie, and even as it hath taught you, ye shall abide in him. **(1 John 2:26,27)**

If you're going to win in this life-if you're going to experience true zoe life that enables you to be victorious-it's vital you understand three things:

(1) "Christ" means "the Anointed One and His anointing. If you are in Christ and Christ is in you, then you are anointed and the Anointed One is in you.

(2) There are antichrists at work in the earth. These are demonic forces whose sole mission is to rob you of the anointing of God.

(3) You have an unction or anointing within you. That anointing causes you to "know all things" you need to know to get to where God has destined you to go.

CHAPTER 2

THE ANOINTING FOR ABUNDANT LIFE

The thief cometh not, but for to steal, and to kill, and to destroy: I am come that they might have life, and that they might have it more abundantly. (John 10:10)

Most people on the earth today aren't truly *living*–they're merely surviving. Tragically, this is almost as true for believers as well.

Far too many Christians know little or nothing of the abundant life Jesus said He came to bring us in John 10:10. The Greek word Jesus used in that scripture is the same word for "life" we studied in the previous chapter. That word is *zoe.*

Zoe life is life on a higher dimension. It is life that is eternal, victorious, powerful and rich. And as we discovered in 1 John, chapter two, we receive *zoe* life by abiding in the anointing:

But ye have an unction [anointing] from the Holy One, and ye know all things...And this is the promise that he hath promised us, even eternal [zoe] life. (1 John 2:20,25)

Do you see the relationship? *Zoe* life is life that results from the anointing. It is only when we live and act under the anointing that we will experience the God-kind of life. With the anointing you can break through all the limitations of the flesh and the natural realm. Instead of being limited by your natural ability, you operate in supernatural power.

This anointing, child of God, is not given just to provide miraculous manifestations in church services. Sure, the anointing will bring miracles when believers get together, and I thank God for those kinds of manifestations, but that's not the primary purpose for the anointing.

11

The anointing is primarily provided to equip you to live a quality of life that is far above and beyond what those in the natural world can experience. That's *zoe* life.

The Anointing of Multiplication

We find one of the great examples of the Anointed One and His anointing bringing life and blessing in John, chapter six. It's the account of Jesus feeding the five thousand:

When Jesus then lifted up his eyes, and saw a great company come unto him, he saith unto Philip, Whence shall we buy bread, that these may eat? And this he said to prove him: for he himself knew what he would do. Philip answered him, Two hundred pennyworth of bread is not sufficient for them, that every one of them may take a little. (John 6:5-7)

The disciples found themselves with some pretty tremendous needs that day. Philip's first instinct was to think of the need in financial terms. He basically said, "Jesus, 200 pennyworth (the equivelant of eight months wages) of food would not be enough to feed this crowd, even a tiny bit of food!"

Andrew, on the other hand saw the problem a little differently, but still didn't understand the significance of the anointing:

One of his disciples, Andrew, Simon Peter's brother, saith unto him, There is a lad here, which hath five barley loaves, and two small fishes: but what are they among so many? (John 6:8-9)

Both Philip and Andrew are looking at the situation through natural eyes. All the while the Anointed One is standing next to them ready to bring *zoe* life into the picture:

And Jesus said, Make the men sit down. Now there was much grass in the place. So the men sat down, in number about five thousand. And Jesus took the loaves; and when he had given thanks, he distributed to the disciples, and the disciples to them that were set down; and likewise of the fishes as much as they would. When they were filled, he said unto his disciples, Gather up the fragments that remain, that nothing be lost. **(John 6:10-12)**

The phrase in this passage I want you to focus in on is, "And Jesus took the loaves..."

You see, for the anointing of multiplication to be applied to your life, you must cause what you have to pass through the hands of Jesus. How do we do that today? Through obedience in tithes and offerings.

Until those fish and loaves were handed over to Jesus, the Anointed One, they remained woefully inadequate to meet the need. But once they came into contact with Jesus, the anointing of multiplication was applied and the need was super-abundantly met!

Therefore they gathered them together, and filled twelve baskets with the fragments of the five barley loaves, which remained over and above unto them that had eaten. **(John 6:13)**

This same principle applies to the area of your finances and material needs today. As long as you are clinging to the little bit you have-withholding God's tithe and never allowing the Spirit of God to speak to you about giving offerings-the anointing of multiplication can't be applied to your resources.

It may surprise you to discover that, often, when you're faced with a financial shortfall, the answer you need is not really money. A lack of *money* is not really the root of the problem. A lack of *the anointing* is the problem.

Lack and insufficiency come when you allow antichrists to drive the anointing of God from your life. You let fear or selfishness cause you to withhold the tithe or cut back on your offerings and before you know it, the anointing has dried up.

Then, you begin to think your answer is money when what you really need is to get the anointing operating in your life once more. Once you do that, money will take care of itself. You'll have the anointing of multiplication working in your

13

material resources.

Don't get upset when you hear a man or woman of God encouraging you to give of your finances. God's not trying to separate you from your money. He's trying to get you to hand it over to Jesus so the anointing of multiplication can be transferred to it.

It's the same principle we see operating in the Old Testament in the account of Elijah and the widow of Zarephath:

So he [Elijah] arose and went to Zarephath. And when he came to the gate of the city, behold, the widow woman was there gathering of sticks: and he called to her, and said, Fetch me, I pray thee, a little water in a vessel, that I may drink. And as she was going to fetch it, he called to her, and said, Bring me, I pray thee, a morsel of bread in thine hand. And she said, As the LORD thy God liveth, I have not a cake, but an handful of meal in a barrel, and a little oil in a cruse: and, behold, I am gathering two sticks, that I may go in and dress it for me and my son, that we may eat it, and die. **(1 Kings 17:10-12)**

This woman was down to her last bit of groceries in a time of famine. She was about to prepare a final meal for herself and her son before they began the long, slow process of starving to death. So, what does God do? He sends them a preacher to whom they can give an offering!

And Elijah said unto her, Fear not; go and do as thou hast said: but make me thereof a little cake first, and bring it unto me, and after make for thee and for thy son. For thus saith the LORD God of Israel, The barrel of meal shall not waste, neither shall the cruse of oil fail, until the day that the LORD sendeth rain upon the earth. **(1 Kings 17:13,14)**

God wanted to help this woman and her son, but He could only do it if she would turn loose of some of her stuff in order to get the anointing of multiplication on it.

Unlike many believers today, this woman had enough faith

in the Word of the Lord to give, even in her need. The results speak for themselves:

And she went and did according to the saying of Elijah: and she, and he, and her house, did eat many days. And the barrel of meal wasted not, neither did the cruse of oil fail, according to the word of the LORD, which he spake by Elijah. **(1 Kings 17:15-16)**

I can just hear the religious folks of today if they had been there in Elijah's time. "Would you look at that? That preacher ought to be ashamed of himself... taking that poor widow woman's last meal!"

People like that don't understand the power of the anointing. God created the principle of sowing and reaping for the very purpose of giving us the ability to put our material goods into Jesus' hands, so we can get the anointing involved.

The next time you sense the Spirit of God prompting you to give, don't get grieved, get excited. God is presenting you with an opportunity to get the anointing of multiplication working in your finances.

There are some things, however, that can hinder the effectiveness of that anointing. Beginning in the next chapter we're going to examine some of the most dangerous ones.

CHAPTER 3

UNHOLY ALLIANCES

"Woe to the obstinate children," declares the LORD, "to those who carry out plans that are not mine, forming an alliance, but not by my Spirit...(Isaiah 30:1 NIV)

If you look across the entire scope of scripture, you'll see that God has always been emphatic on one particular point. He has always warned His people to avoid unholy alliances.

In Deuteronomy, chapter 17, Moses warned Israel against ever "going down to Egypt for horses." He was referring to the temptation to someday look to the pagan nation of Egypt for military support and assistance. He was telling them to avoid unholy alliances.

Centuries later Solomon violated this command and it led to his downfall and the downfall of Israel. We read about it in 1 Kings:

Then Solomon formed a marriage alliance with Pharaoh king of Egypt, and took Pharaoh's daughter and brought her to the city of David. **(1 Kings 3:1 NASB)**

Even "good King Jehoshaphat" fell victim to this kind of error:

And after this Jehoshaphat king of Judah allied himself with Ahaziah king of Israel. He acted wickedly in so doing. **(2 Chronicles 20:35 NASB)**

The prophet Isaiah summed up how dangerous making unholy alliances can be in this passage:

Woe to those who go down to Egypt for help, And rely on horses, And trust in chariots because they are many, And in horsemen because they are very strong, But they do not look to the Holy One of Israel, nor seek the LORD! **(Isaiah 31:1 NASB)**

That last sentence highlights why these kinds of alliances are so dangerous. They represent a child of God looking to someone or something other than God for help, security or provision. And that is why an unholy alliance is one of the greatest hindrances to the anointing.

"But Brother Dollar, how does that apply to me today?"

I realize that you've probably never personally been tempted to sign a treaty with Egypt or a pagan nation, but the principle is more relevant for us today than ever.

As anointed believers, we must avoid connecting ourselves to any practice, any person or any thing that tends to quench or inhibit the anointing. And we must make sure we're not looking to anything or anyone but God for our sense of security or provision.

That's the spirit behind these familiar verses in Hebrews, chapter 12:

Wherefore seeing we also are compassed about with so great a cloud of witnesses, let us lay aside every weight, and the sin which doth so easily beset us, and let us run with patience the race that is set before us, Looking unto Jesus the author and finisher of our faith; **(Hebrews 12:1-2)**

Laying aside weights and sins is another way of saying "break all the unholy alliances that tend to hinder the anointing." Instead we are directed to focus our attention on Jesus, the Anointed One and His anointing.

Now lets take a look at some of the most common unholy alliances that hinder the anointing.

Growing Up in the Anointing

Throughout the book of Ephesians, the Apostle Paul repeatedly talks about what it means to be "in Christ." Another way of saying "in Christ" would be "in the Anointed

One and His anointing."

In the first chapter alone, the phrase "in Christ" occurs five times.

Then, in chapter four, the Apostle Paul talks about how the Church has been given the five-fold ministry gifts (apostle, prophet, evangelist, pastor and teacher), and that those gifts are going to operate until "we all come in the unity of the faith, and of the knowledge of the Son of God, unto a perfect man, unto the measure of the stature of the fulness of Christ." (Ephesians 4:13)

In other words, these ministry gifts are designed to help the church grow up into the full measure of "the Anointed One and His anointing."

A couple of verses later, Paul once again tells us, "It's time to grow up:"

That we henceforth be no more children, tossed to and fro, and carried about with every wind of doctrine, by the sleight of men, and cunning craftiness, whereby they lie in wait to deceive; But speaking the truth in love, may grow up into him in all things, which is the head, even Christ [the Anointed One and His anointing]: **(Ephesians 4:14-15)**

A few verses later Paul begins to list some things that hinder that anointing. We find the first of these in Ephesians 4:25:

Wherefore putting away lying, speak every man truth with his neighbour: for we are members one of another.

An unholy alliance with deceit is a major hindrance to the anointing. Sadly, enormous numbers of believers have developed a comfortable relationship with lying. In fact, for many Christians, lying has become a lifestyle.

In the next verse we find another deadly enemy of the anointing-sinful anger.

Be ye angry, and sin not: let not the sun go down upon your wrath. Neither give place to the devil. **(Ephesians 4:26-27)**

19

There is a time and a place for anger, (particularly anger at the devil and at sin) but when you let anger at another person fester and linger, in other words, when you "let the sun go down" on it, you're "giving place to the devil." Another translation says,"do not give the devil an opportunity." (NASB)

You can count on one thing-the devil is constantly looking for an opportunity to bring death, destruction and misery to your life. First Peter 5:8 says it this way:

Be sober, be vigilant; because your adversary the devil, as a roaring lion, walketh about, seeking whom he may devour:

One of the surest ways to give the devil an opportunity in your life is to let hurt or anger turn into bitterness. Develop an unholy alliance with anger and you'll quench the anointing and leave a hole in your defenses so wide the devil can drive a truckload of burdens and yokes through it.

A third unholy alliance that will destroy your anointing is found in the next verse of Ephesians, chapter four:

Let him that stole steal no more: but rather let him labour, working with his hands the thing which is good, that he may have to give to him that needeth. **(Ephesians 4:28)**

Have you developed a relationship with stealing? "Not me!" you say, "I'm not a thief."

Hold on just a minute before you get too confident in that assertion. Do you ever goof off on the job? Do you permit your employer to pay you for time you didn't work? When a cashier accidentally gives you too much change, do you keep it?

There are a lot more ways to steal than just walking out of a department store without paying for something.

Millions of Christians today are guilty of the worst kind of thievery of all-stealing from God Himself. How do you steal from God? Ask the prophet Malachi:

Will a man rob God? <u>*Yet ye have robbed me.*</u> *But ye say, Wherein have we robbed thee?* <u>*In tithes and offerings.*</u> *Ye are cursed with a curse: for ye have robbed me, even this whole nation.* (Malachi 3:8-9)

When you fall into a lifestyle of stealing-whether at work or at church, you develop an unholy alliance with something that will greatly hinder the anointing and all the wonderful things it brings into your life.

The next verse highlights a fourth hindrance to the anointing:

Let no corrupt communication proceed out of your mouth, but that which is good to the use of edifying, that it may minister grace unto the hearers. And grieve not the holy Spirit of God, whereby ye are sealed unto the day of redemption. (Ephesians 4:29-30)

Far too many believers have a problem with this thing the Bible calls "corrupt communication."

Keep in mind, it's not merely talking about using curse words or foul language. "Corrupt communication" is any speech that is worthless or counter to the Word of God.

If you're murmuring, complaining, criticizing or talking about your problems, your communication is corrupt and, according to the verse we just read, you're in danger of grieving the Holy Ghost.

That's why an unholy alliance with corrupt communication is such a hindrance to the anointing. The anointing is of the Holy Spirit and worthless negative talk grieves Him!

Jesus confirmed this truth in Matthew, chapter 12:

A good man out of the good treasure of the heart bringeth forth good things: and an evil man out of the evil treasure bringeth forth evil things. But I say unto you, That every idle word that men shall speak, they shall give account thereof in the day of judgment. For by thy words thou shalt be justified, and by thy words thou shalt be condemned. (Matthew 12:35-37)

Examine your speech. If there are traces of corrupt communication, break that unholy alliance now. The anointing is too precious and too vital to compromise through worthless talk.

There are many more relationships and alliances that can

keep you from experiencing all the blessing, protection and provision the anointing brings and we'll be examining some of these in the coming chapters.

At this point it's just important to purpose and say in your heart, "I'll not allow unholy alliances to hinder my anointing."

Making a quality decision like that will take you a long way towards living the abundant life Jesus died to bring you.

CHAPTER 4

CONSTRAINED BY THE LOVE OF THE ANOINTING

For the love of Christ constraineth us; because we thus judge, that if one died for all, then were all dead: **(2 Corinthians 5:14)**

"The love of Christ (the Anointed One and His anointing) constrains us." That's an amazing statement the Apostle Paul makes. It's a statement that has come to mean more and more to me the longer I meditate on it.

We don't use the word "constrain" much in our modern English, but it's a powerful word with a specific meaning.

To constrain means "to arrest or compel." And that is precisely what a love for the anointing will do in your life. It will arrest you or compel you to stop when you're about to do something that will violate or quench the anointing.

Once you've been anointed-once you've experienced the power, joy and freedom it brings-you'll never want to live another moment without it. A love for the anointing of the Spirit of God will compel you not to forge unholy alliances with the enemies of that anointing.

How do you cultivate a love for the anointing? Well, you can't love something you don't know anything about. Getting to know the Anointed One, Jesus, and learning more about the anointing He brings, will deepen your love for them both (and remember, you can't separate the two-the Anointed One and His anointing are all tied up and tangled up together)!

The reason many believers are never constrained or arrested before they enter into an unholy alliance is they've never gotten to know the anointing well enough to value it

23

over their sin, habit, comfort or religious tradition.

That's why, in Ephesians chapter three, Paul says his earnest desire is that his readers would get a full understanding of the love of Christ, the Anointed One and His anointing:

That Christ [the Anointed One and His anointing] may dwell in your hearts by faith; that ye, being rooted and grounded in love, May be able to comprehend with all saints what is the breadth, and length, and depth, and height; And to know the love of [the Anointed One and His anointing], which passeth knowledge, that ye might be filled with all the fulness of God. (Ephesians 3:17-19)

Paul knew that if the Ephesians could cultivate a love of the anointing-a love that went beyond knowledge-everything else in life would take care of itself. He knew a love for the anointing would prevent the Ephesians from experiencing the death, destruction, and heartache unholy alliances bring.

Connections Count

What the Word of God is trying to communicate to us through everything I've been saying can be boiled down to this statement: Connections count. The people and things we connect ourselves to through relationship, meditation, habit or thought, have a huge impact on our lives because they impact our level of anointing. And as we've seen, only the anointing of God has the power to remove burdens and destroy yokes.

This is exactly what Paul was saying in the following verse:

Be ye not unequally yoked together with unbelievers: for what fellowship hath righteousness with unrighteous-ness? and what communion hath light with darkness? (2 Corinthians 6:14)

Isn't that a clear warning against unholy alliances? The words "fellowship" and "communion" that Paul uses here are relationship words. The Greek word translated "fellowship" is *metoche.* It literally means "intercourse."

The word translated "communion" is the Greek word,

koinonia. It refers to a tight, affectionate, giving and taking kind of relationship.

Now allow me to paraphrase the questions Paul asked in the above verse: "What business does an anointed believer have engaging in intercourse and close relationship with dark forces of unrighteousness?" The answer of course is, "NONE!"

Paul goes on to ask some similar questions in the next few verses:

And what concord hath Christ with Belial [the worthless one]? or what part hath he that believeth with an infidel? And what agreement hath the temple of God with idols?... **(2 Corinthians 6:15-16a)**

Then the Word goes on to tell us why it is such an abomination for an anointed child of God to have these kinds of unholy alliances:

...for ye are the temple of the living God; as God hath said, I will dwell in them, and walk in them; and I will be their God, and they shall be my people. **(2 Corinthians 6:16b)**

Do you see it? Do you understand why unholy alliances are so destructive to the presence of the anointing in your life? It's because that anointing represents God Himself on the inside of you. You are the "temple of the living God!"

The very next verse gives clear instructions concerning these unholy relationships, AND a promise if we obey:

Wherefore come out from among them, and be ye separate, saith the Lord, and touch not the unclean thing; and I will receive you, And will be a Father unto you, and ye shall be my sons and daughters, saith the Lord Almighty. **(2 Corinthians 6:17-18)**

God is saying, "If you'll judge yourself where unholy alliances are concerned, I'm going to receive you and treat you like a favored child."

There are some things God wants to do in you, through

you and for you, but they can only be done in the presence of the anointing. Therefore, you must "come out" from relationships with unholy things and be separate.

"Now look at the next two verses, there's something important I want you to see:

Having therefore these promises, dearly beloved, let us cleanse ourselves from all filthiness of the flesh and spirit, perfecting holiness in the fear of God. Receive us; we have wronged no man, we have corrupted no man, we have defrauded no man. (2 Corinthians 7:1-2)

Brother Kenneth Copeland talks about the time he was reading the above verse in which Paul says, "We have wronged no man." When he came to that part he stopped and said, "Lord, I just caught Paul in a lie."

Brother Copeland knew from reading the book of Acts that Paul, when he was known as Saul of Tarsus, had been personally involved in the persecution, imprisonment and even execution of Christians. He wondered, "How then, could Paul claim he had wronged no one?"

Then the Lord spoke to his spirit and said, "The man that did those things died on the road to Damascus."

The Lord was pointing out a truth that Paul understood very well. Just two chapters prior to the one we've been studying Paul wrote: Therefore if any man be in Christ, he is a new creature: old things are passed away; behold, all things are become new. (2 Corinthians 5:17)

In his conversion experience on the road to Damascus, Paul broke free from all unholy alliances. The same can be true for you and me.

You may have been the vilest person in the state. You may have been involved in unspeakable things. But if you are "in Christ" today-if you've made Jesus the Lord of your life-all that old stuff is dead and buried and so is the person who did them. You are a new creation.

God is now your ally and you're connected to Him by the Holy Spirit and His anointing.

CHAPTER 5

CONTAGIOUS ATTITUDES
AND THE ANOINTING

Have this attitude in yourselves which was also in Christ Jesus... **(Philippians 2:5 NASB)**

Attitudes just don't appear full grown in a moment of time. Attitudes, good and bad, are fed, nurtured and developed over time. Whenever I come across someone with a really rotten attitude about something, I know that someone, somewhere along the line has been feeding it. It didn't just "happen."

This is a truth that is important to remember because a relationship with a bad attitude can be one of those unholy alliances we've been talking about. And attitudes are highly contagious.

A classic example of someone in the Bible who caught an unholy attitude is found in the book of Numbers:

And Miriam and Aaron spake against Moses because of the Ethiopian woman whom he had married: for he had married an Ethiopian woman. **(Numbers 12:1)**

Miriam was Moses' sister and Aaron was his brother. Here we find them beginning to grumble against Moses because they didn't care for the person he married. Apparently, one of them started with an attitude and the other one caught it.

A little later in the account we find out who the instigator of this little rebellion was. What was the nature of this unholy attitude? Jealousy and pride.

And they said, Hath the LORD indeed spoken only by Moses? hath he not spoken also by us? <u>And the LORD heard it.</u> **(Numbers 12:2)**

There's one thing I want you to notice about this ugly talk Miriam and Aaron were participating in-"the Lord heard it." You can be sure that whenever you're running your mouth, the Lord is hearing.

We've seen in a previous chapter how idle words and corrupt communication are hindrances to the anointing. Now we're going to see how seriously God takes these kinds of unholy alliances:

(Now the man Moses was very meek, above all the men which were upon the face of the earth.) And the LORD spake suddenly unto Moses, and unto Aaron, and unto Miriam, Come out ye three unto the tabernacle of the congregation. And they three came out. And the LORD came down in the pillar of the cloud, and stood in the door of the tabernacle, and called Aaron and Miriam: and they both came forth. **(Numbers 12:3-5)**

The Lord takes the anointing very seriously. Moses was His anointed and these two were daring to touch and attack that anointing with their words and attitudes. God had something to say about it:

And he said, Hear now my words: If there be a prophet among you, I the LORD will make myself known unto him in a vision, and will speak unto him in a dream. My servant Moses is not so, who is faithful in all mine house. With him will I speak mouth to mouth, even apparently, and not in dark speeches; and the similitude of the LORD shall he behold: wherefore then were ye not afraid to speak against my servant Moses? **(Numbers 12:6-8)**

God was saying, "I usually only speak to prophets in dreams and visions, but my anointing is so heavy on Moses because of his faithfulness, that I speak to him face to face. Why then were you not afraid to speak against Him?"

God is serious about this stuff. That's why, in First Chronicles 16:22, He says, "Touch not mine anointed, and do my prophets no harm." So, when Miriam and Aaron connected in an unholy alliance with gossip, slander and strife, they discovered they had the Almighty One to answer to:

And the anger of the LORD was kindled against them; and he departed. And the cloud departed from off the tabernacle; and, behold, Miriam became leprous, white as snow: and Aaron looked upon Miriam, and, behold, she was leprous. **(Numbers 12:9-10)**

Now we know who originally had the unholy alliance. Miriam, by meditating and pondering on all the attention Moses was getting, developed a relationship with jealousy. Then Aaron caught her attitude and connected with the same vile spirit.

I've seen something similar happen in my church. A while back someone got offended because they thought I was preaching too much on tithing. They went around talking about it and looking for people who would agree with them.

In a few vulnerable folks that attitude was contagious, and they made the same connection with that unholy alliance. Before long about a dozen people left the church.

Well, as it turned out, that month was one of the greatest months of growth we've ever had as a church. In fact, I jokingly told my wife, "My Lord, let's hire that woman to come in here about it once a quarter, and see how many people she can lead off. We'll be the largest church in America in less than a year!"

All kidding aside, you have to be diligent about what you listen to and who you let plant thoughts and ideas into your mind and heart.

There are people out there with poisonous attitudes and they're contagious. But if you do catch one, it's good to know the Lord is merciful and quick to forgive and restore. Miriam and Aaron repented and Miriam was subsequently healed and restored.

The Cure for Contagious Attitudes

In the third chapter of Colossians is a powerful set of verses about the Anointed One and His anointing. They talk about what we need to do to stay connected with the anointing and stay free of unholy alliances. Look at the first verse, for example:

If ye then be risen with Christ [the Anointed One and His anointing], seek those things which are above, where [the Anointed One] sitteth on the right hand of God. Set your affection on things above, not on things on the earth. For ye are dead, and your life is hid with [the Anointed One] in God. (Colossians 3:1-3)

We're told to set our affections on those things which are above.

The root of the word "affection" is "affect." When you have an affection for something, it changes you-it *affects* you.

We're told to let that which is above, the Anointed One and His anointing, change us, rather than allowing the dead things of the earth to move us.

When your thoughts, meditations, plans, hopes and dreams center on the Anointed One, who is, above and His anointing, which is upon you, you'll stay free of unholy alliances and you won't be infected by contagious attitudes.

CHAPTER 6

SEDUCTIONS AGAINST THE ANOINTING

Now the Spirit speaketh expressly, that in the latter times some shall depart from the faith, giving heed to seducing spirits, and doctrines of devils; **(1 Timothy 4:1)**

For most of this book, we've been examining spiritual forces and earthly things that work to hinder the burden-removing, yoke-destroying power of the anointing in your life. We've looked at antichrists, unholy alliances and contagious attitudes. In each case we've seen how destructive these forces can be.

Now, before you start thinking that this entire book is going to focus on the negative, let me assure you that we're getting ready to examine the powerful, positive aspects of the anointing and how you can cultivate them in your life. But before we do, there is one more trap that the enemy has laid for you of which I need to make you aware. It is a trap to draw you away from the anointing.

The Bible calls this trap seduction.

The Word of God warns us about seduction and seducing spirits in several places. One warning is found in First John, chapter two:

These things have I written unto you concerning them that seduce you. But the anointing which ye have received of him abideth in you... **(1 John 2:26,27)**

Here John tells us that steering clear of seduction is directly tied to abiding in the anointing.

The bottom line is: there is a spirit of seduction which will

31

try to draw and lure you into unholy alliances.

In every seduction there must, by necessity, be two parties- a seducer and a seducee. Without both parties present and cooperating, no seduction can take place.

Why, then is seduction into unholy alliances so common? Because these two elements are like magnets. They attract one another.

There is often a spiritual connection that takes place between someone who is susceptible to being seduced away from the anointing and the things of God, and someone sent by Satan as a seducer.

Here's a warning: If you allow one of these seducers, John is warning us about, to get you connected in an unholy alliance of some sort, it will choke off the flow of the anointing in your life.

Seduction in the Garden

As a matter of fact, it was a seduction that brought sin, death, yokes and burdens into the world in the first place. We see this clearly in Genesis, chapter three:

Now the serpent was more subtil than any beast of the field which the LORD God had made. And he said unto the woman, Yea, hath God said, Ye shall not eat of every tree of the garden? **(Genesis 3:1)**

Notice that the serpent was "subtle." We need to be careful about subtle things. Not every trap comes walking up to you with a big, flashing neon sign shouting "I'm a trap!" Many pitfalls are subtle.

A thing doesn't have to be a full manifestation of evil before you start putting up your guard. If you're engaged in a seemingly innocent conversation with someone and you get a little warning in your spirit, don't disregard it. The Spirit of God is probably trying to warn you of a subtle approach from the enemy.

In the case of Eve, the serpent began by trying to get her to question the Word of God.

God's Word of instruction concerning the trees of the garden had been clear. "Eat of any tree you like except this one." Now the devil has come and wants Eve to question the integrity of the Word.

And the woman said unto the serpent, We may eat of the fruit of the trees of the garden: But of the fruit of the tree which is in the midst of the garden, God hath said, Ye shall not eat of it, neither shall ye touch it, lest ye die. **(Genesis 3:2-3)**

Eve's words here are basically true. But her mistake was in responding at all. Instead of walking away, she is now engaging a seducing spirit in conversation. By establishing a relationship, she is opening herself to deception and the creation of an unholy alliance.

Of course, now that he's been given an opportunity, the serpent openly questions the truth and validity of the Word of the Lord:

And the serpent said unto the woman, Ye shall not surely die: For God doth know that in the day ye eat thereof, then your eyes shall be opened, and ye shall be as gods, knowing good and evil. **(Genesis 3:4-5)**

Not only does the serpent question the truth of the Word here, he goes on to question God's character! He says, "The only reason God doesn't want you to eat this fruit is because He knows that when you do, you'll become like Him."

Look at how this seduction is progressing. It's starts with a casual conversation. Then the seducer gets you questioning the Word. Then he gets you to question God's integrity. The next step is always an appeal to the lust of your flesh, the lust of your eyes, or the boastful pride of life. (1 John 2:16) Look at the very next verse:

And when the woman saw that the tree was good for food [lust of the flesh], and that it was pleasant to the eyes [lust of the eyes], and a tree to be desired to make one wise [the boastful pride of life], she took of the fruit thereof, and did eat, and gave also unto her husband with her; and he did eat. **(Genesis 3:6)**

Now the seduction is complete. The only thing left is to begin to realize the tragic consequences of having lost the anointing. For Adam and Eve that anointing had provided a covering of glory. Now it was gone.

And the eyes of them both were opened, and they knew that they were naked; and they sewed fig leaves together, and made themselves aprons. **(Genesis 3:7)**

Those fig leaf aprons are symbolic of religion. People always get religious when they are seduced and lose the anointing. Instead of a covering of anointed glory, they sew themselves a covering of religious works.

But there's one thing religion can't do-restore your confidence before God. Now that Adam and Eve had been seduced, they found themselves trembling and hiding from God's presence rather than enjoying the sweetness of His fellowship.

And they heard the voice of the LORD God walking in the garden in the cool of the day: and Adam and his wife hid themselves from the presence of the LORD God amongst the trees of the garden. And the LORD God called unto Adam, and said unto him, Where art thou? And he said, I heard thy voice in the garden, and I was afraid, because I was naked; and I hid myself. **(Genesis 3:8-10)**

You can't be involved in an unholy alliance and feel comfortable in the presence of the Lord. You'll flee from that presence. You'll stop reading the Word. You'll stop spending time in prayer. You'll find excuses not to go to church. Instead of enjoying the fellowship of the Lord, you'll shrink back from His presence.

Of course, nothing is hidden from God's eyes. He always knows what we've been doing:

And he said, Who told thee that thou wast naked? Hast thou eaten of the tree, whereof I commanded thee that thou shouldest not eat? **(Genesis 3:11)**

Notice that God asked, "Who told you...?" You see, God recognized that Adam and Eve's loss of the anointing had to be the result of an unholy alliance. There had to be a unholy relationship at the root of the seduction.

Of course, at that point, the finger pointing began:

And the man said, The woman whom thou gavest to be with me, she gave me of the tree, and I did eat. And the LORD God said unto the woman, What is this that thou hast done? And the woman said, The serpent beguiled me, and I did eat. **(Gen 3:12-13)**

If you're ever going to be free-if you're ever going to walk in the fullness of the anointing-you're going to have to get to the root of the things that hinder the anointing. Those roots are always unholy alliances.

A Hindrance to Hearing God

We see another example of seduction into unholy alliances when we examine the lives of Abram and his nephew, Lot. Abram's story begins with him receiving a direct order from God:

Now the LORD had said unto Abram, Get thee out of thy country, and from thy kindred, and from thy father's house, unto a land that I will show thee: **(Genesis 12:1)**

Now notice God's specific instructions here. Abram was not to just leave the country but to leave his "kindred" or relatives, too. Did Abram obey those instructions to the letter? Read verse four to find out:

So Abram departed, as the LORD had spoken unto him; and Lot went with him: **(Genesis 12:4)**

God had important plans for Abram. In order for those plans to be accomplished, Abram needed to break all unholy alliances. That's why God instructed him to leave all his pagan kinfolk behind. The Lord knew that those relationships would hinder the anointing in Abram's life.

Sure enough, a little later on we see this unholy alliance beginning to bear evil fruit:

And there was a strife between the herdmen of Abram's cattle and the herdmen of Lot's cattle: **(Genesis 13:7)**

The strife that resulted from an unholy alliance almost kept Abram from fulfilling his divine destiny. Ultimately, however, Abram and Lot went their separate ways.

As soon as Abram got back into obedience by breaking the connection that was hindering his anointing, he got back on track with God's plan. Look at how Abraham's ability to hear from God was restored as soon as he broke the tie with Lot:

And the LORD said unto Abram, after that Lot was separated from him, Lift up now thine eyes, and look from the place where thou art northward, and southward, and eastward, and westward: For all the land which thou seest, to thee will I give it, and to thy seed for ever. **(Genesis 13:14-15)**

If it's been a while since you've heard the Lord speaking to you, maybe it's because an unholy alliance has dulled your ears to the voice of God.

If you don't seem to be making progress in your calling or toward your God-given dreams, it may be that you've been seduced into a relationship that keeps you from reaching your destiny.

That seduction may have come through the lust of the flesh, the lust of the eyes or the boastful pride of life. But whatever channel it came through, it will stop you from reaching your destiny if you don't take steps to correct it.

It's vital that each of us learn to judge ourselves if we are to stay free of these relationships and connections that keep us back.

Child of God, I have good news for you today. God has sent the Anointed One and His anointing and in these last days, those of us who know who we are in Christ are going to live lives free from seduction. We will not yield to unholy alliances. We'll be able to stand in the middle of hell itself and shout, "Devil, you can't affect me. You can't seduce me. I know who I am, and I'm anointed!"

CHAPTER 7

THE ANOINTING AND THE BLOOD

And there are three that bear witness in earth, the spirit, and the water, and the blood: and these three agree in one. (1 John 5:8)

There is a relationship between the anointing and the blood of Jesus. This is a truth I haven't heard taught much in Christian circles but it holds a vital key to growing and living in the burden-removing, yoke-destroying power of God.

It may seem unusual, but a good place to start a study of this truth is in the last book of the Bible. Let's take a look at Revelation 12:9:

And the great dragon was cast out, that old serpent, called the Devil, and Satan, which deceiveth the whole world: he was cast out into the earth, and his angels were cast out with him.

This verse gives us a behind-the-scenes glimpse into the realm of the spirit at the time when Lucifer and his co-rebels were cast out of heaven.

Now, notice what takes place immediately after this cataclysmic heavenly event:

And I heard a loud voice saying in heaven, Now is come salvation, and strength, and the kingdom of our God, and the power of his Christ: for the accuser of our brethren is cast down, which accused them before our God day and night. (Revelation 12:10)

If we translate that statement, as we have learned to do, it would read something like, "Now is come salvation, and strength, and the kingdom of our God, *and the power of His Anointed One and His anointing.*"

Isn't it interesting that we see an announcement of the power of the anointing right after we see Satan being cast down to the earth? Why is that? Because the anointing is "the burden-removing, yoke-destroying power of God," and until the devil came on the scene, there weren't any burdens or yokes!

We get more insight into this spiritual battle in the very next verse:

And they overcame him by the blood of the Lamb, and by the word of their testimony; and they loved not their lives unto the death. **(Revelation 12:11)**

That verse is a familiar one for most of us. We hear a lot about "overcoming by the blood." Phrases such as "pleading the blood," and "Satan, the blood of Jesus is against you," are common among Christians.

But what do we really mean when we say these things? How and why do we overcome by the blood? What does it really mean to "plead" the blood and how do you do it? Why is there "power, power, wonder-working power" in the blood?

Over the next few chapters we'll find answers to these questions and while we're at it, we'll discover the reason for the link we just saw between the anointing and the blood.

The Purpose of Shed Blood

There has been a lot of blood shed in this earth over the last 6,000 years. Some of it has been shed for valid reasons. Much of it has not.

When an animal is killed to provide food, it's blood is shed with a purpose. But we have no right to kill animals just for the sake of killing. This is bloodshed without a purpose.

This gives us an important key: For blood to be shed legitimately, it must be shed for a purpose.

That brings us to a larger question. Why was Jesus' blood shed? What was the purpose?

The answer is tightly tied in with what we see in the Old Testament regarding the sacrifice of animals for the covering of sin and in the shedding of an animal's blood in cutting blood covenant.

You most likely remember the account in Genesis of God cutting covenant with Abraham by cutting animals in half and walking between the pieces.

You're also probably aware of how the Old Testament priests, per God's instructions, would slaughter bulls, goats and lambs and sprinkle the blood on the mercy seat to atone for the sins of the people.

It is with these Old Covenant practices in mind that the writer of Hebrews teaches us about the blood of Christ in the New Covenant. Look, for example at some enlightening verses in Hebrews, chapter nine:

Now when these things [the Old Covenant sacrifices] have been thus prepared, the priests are continually entering the outer tabernacle, performing the divine worship, but into the second [the Holy of Holies] only the high priest enters, once a year, not without taking blood, which he offers for himself and for the sins of the people committed in ignorance. **(Hebrews 9:6-7 NASB)**

In Old Testament Israel, the High Priest would offer sacricies once a year for all the sins of the people. For that sacrifice to be effective, they had to *believe* that the blood of the animal sprinkled on the mercy seat would be acceptable to God to cover their sins.

In other words, there was an element of *faith* required to be in right standing with God. There was really no power in the blood of the bulls. The power was in the people's faith in God's statement that He would accept it. You can fill a swimming pool full of blood, but without the faith in what God said about it, there is no covering of sin.

It wasn't the blood itself that mattered. It was what that blood accomplished.

The same is true for us today. Those Old Covenant sacrifices merely foreshadowed what Jesus would ultimately have to do to redeem mankind.

That's exactly what we're told later on in the same passage we just read:

> *But when Christ appeared as a high priest of the good things to come, He entered through the greater and more perfect tabernacle, not made with hands, that is to say, not of this creation; and not through the blood of goats and calves, but through His own blood, He entered the holy place once for all, having obtained eternal redemption. For if the blood of goats and bulls and the ashes of a heifer sprinkling those who have been defiled, sanctify for the cleansing of the flesh, how much more will the blood of Christ, who through the eternal Spirit offered Himself without blemish to God, cleanse your conscience from dead works to serve the living God?* **(Hebrews 9:11-14 NASB)**

Today, it is our faith in the fact that God accepted Jesus' precious, holy blood that cleanses our consciences. We see a similar thought in Romans, chapter three:

> *Christ Jesus: Whom God hath set forth to be a propitiation [sacrificial substitute] through faith in his blood, to declare his righteousness for the remission of sins that are past, through the forbearance of God;* **(Romans 3:24b, 25)**

The Anointed Jesus can only be your atoning sacrifice "through faith in His blood." And part of having faith in the blood is knowing what that blood has done for you. To remain in ignorance concerning what the blood of Jesus accomplished for you is to limit the power of that blood in your life.

Understanding the Power of the Blood

Many believers have a fuzzy sort of faith in the blood because they have a very limited understanding of what Jesus' blood accomplished.

They'll stand up in church and sing, *"What can wash away my sins? Nothing but the blood of Jesus,"* and shout "Amen!" But turn around and ask them, "Are you righteous?," and they'll piously say, "Oh, no brother. There is none righteous, no not one."

Well, which is it? Does the blood wash away your sins or doesn't it? Do you see what I'm saying? Many of us have contradictory concepts in our minds when it comes to what the blood has done for us.

This is why Christians with only a limited understanding of redemption can "plead the blood" until they're blue in the face and never see any results.

You can shout "Satan, the blood of Jesus is against you," from now until Jesus comes back, but it won't send the devil packing unless you know and have faith in what that blood did for you.

To get that kind of understanding, let's go a little bit deeper and discover something vital about the nature of the blood of Jesus.

The Nature of the Blood

What was the nature of that blood that flowed through Jesus' veins? Was it just like your blood and mine? In one way, yes. But in another vitally important way, it was very, very different.

You'll remember that Jesus was born when the Spirit of God came and hovered over the virgin, Mary. As a result, she conceieved of the Holy Ghost.

Now, if you'll refer back to your high school biology, you'll remember that blood type is determined, not by the mother, but by the father.

When a child is in the mother's womb, their blood never mixes or mingles. They have two totally separate blood types and blood systems.

With these two facts in mind we can know that the type and nature of Jesus' blood was determined by His father, God. Mary, as a descendant of Adam, was part of the fallen race of men. But her contaminated blood never mixed with the holy blood flowing through Jesus' veins.

To put it simply, Jesus carried the blood of God Himself.

Jesus became the first man born since Adam to enter the

earth without blood contaminated by sin and death. He didn't have blood type "O" or "B." He had the only type that qualifies you to be a sacrifice for all of man-type "G"-for "God."

Now, ask yourself, when was the first time Jesus' blood was ever shed? It wasn't on the cross. It wasn't when they scourged His back. It wasn't even when they pressed that crown of thorns on His head.

No, we find the first instance of Jesus shedding His blood in Luke, chapter 22:

And he came out, and went, as he was wont, to the mount of Olives; and his disciples also followed him. And when he was at the place, he said unto them, Pray that ye enter not into temptation.   And he was withdrawn from them about a stone's cast, and kneeled down, and prayed, Saying, Father, if thou be willing, remove this cup from me: nevertheless not my will, but thine, be done.   And there appeared an angel unto him from heaven, strengthening him. And being in an agony he prayed more earnestly: and his sweat was as it were great drops of blood falling down to the ground. **(Luke 22:39-44)**

I always used to wonder what was going on here with Jesus sweating out drops of blood. Now I think I understand it.

Throughout the Bible, the shedding of blood is always associated with the cutting of a covenant. I believe God was in the midst of cutting a covenant with Jesus there in the Garden of Gethsemane-a covenant that had to be concealed from Satan at all cost.

The Word tells us that if the devil had known about God's plan for redemption, he never would have had Jesus crucified. We see that in 1 Corinthians 2:7-8:

But we speak the wisdom of God in a mystery, even the hidden wisdom, which God ordained before the world unto our glory: Which none of the princes of this world knew: for had they known it, they would not have crucified the Lord of glory.

God was about to make good on the promise He had made all the way back in the Garden of Eden. That promise was that a seed of the woman would one day crush the head of the serpent. (Genesis 3:15)

Another reason I know a covenant agreement is taking place here is because Jesus talks about a *cup.* He said, *"Father, if thou be willing, remove this cup from me."* **(Luke 22:42a)**

A cup is an instrument of covenant. Covenant meals usually involved a shared cup of wine, sometimes mixed with blood.

At the last supper, Jesus told His disciples, *"This cup is the new testament in my blood, which is shed for you."* **(Luke 22:20b)**

There's something else I want you to notice about the drops of blood Jesus shed there in the garden. They dropped to the ground.

When I read that I'm reminded that God formed man out of the dust of the ground. The blood that fell from Jesus' brow onto the brown earth of the Mount of Olives, would shortly flow from His side in order to restore fallen man to the glory and fellowship with God that Adam forfeited.

What a moment this was. The eternal fate of all of mankind hung in the balance and God the Father and God the Son did business on that hillside.

They made an agreement. Jesus said, "I'll lay down my life and suffer hell itself to redeem mankind." In turn, God said, "I'll accept that sacrifice and call the debt paid."

Then they sealed that holy covenant with a cup and blood.

Oh, child of God, what a wonder. What a precious and mighty thing is the blood of Jesus.

CHAPTER 8

SIN CONSCIOUSNESS AND THE ANOINTING

But God commendeth his love toward us, in that, while we were yet sinners, Christ died for us. Much more then, being now justified by his blood, we shall be saved from wrath through him. (**Romans 5:8-9**)

The above passage of scripture has been used to lead millions to salvation. It's a powerful statement about the love of God and the power of the blood.

It specifically talks about "being justified" by the blood of Jesus. Not many Christians think much about it, but there is an important connection between knowing you're justified and living in the anointing.

What does being justified mean? When you're *justified,* it is *just-as-if* you'd never sinned. As far as God is concerned, you have no right to carry around a sin consciousness.

The next few verses in that passage shed more light on this truth:

For if while we were enemies, we were reconciled to God through the death of His Son, much more, having been reconciled, we shall be saved by His life. And not only this, but we also exult in God through our Lord Jesus Christ, through whom we have now received the reconciliation. (**Romans 5:10-11 NASB**)

Here we learn that being justified also means we get *reconciled* to God.

We were estranged and separated from God by sin. Through disobedience we declared ourselves to be His enemies. But once the blood *justifies* you, it also *reconciles* you to Him. But you have to "receive" that reconciliation.

That's where many believers miss it. They know that, technically, they're forgiven, but they still think God is mad at them. They allow a sin consciousness to keep a wedge between them and God. In other words, they refuse to receive reconciliation.

This is a tremendous hindrance to the anointing. It is difficult for the Holy Ghost to operate freely in your life when you are carrying around an awareness of sins.

Atonement vs Remission

One key to getting rid of a sin consciousness is to get a clear understanding of the concept of remission.

You see, under the old covenant, the sacrifices of bulls and goats made "atonement" for the sins of the people.

And thou shalt offer every day a bullock for a sin offering for atonement: and thou shalt cleanse the altar, when thou hast made an atonement for it, and thou shalt anoint it, to sanctify it. (Exodus 29:36)

To "atone" means to temporarily cover. These Old Testament sacrifices didn't remove the guilt of people's sins, they merely covered them year to year. We get a clear explanation of this truth in Hebrews, chapter ten:

For the Law, since it has only a shadow of the good things to come and not the very form of things, can never by the same sacrifices year by year, which they offer continually, make perfect those who draw near. Otherwise, would they not have ceased to be offered, because the worshipers, having once been cleansed, would no longer have had consciousness of sins? But in those sacrifices there is a reminder of sins year by year. For it is impossible for the blood of bulls and goats to take away sins. (**Hebrews 10:1-4 NASB**)

The writer of Hebrews is telling us that those old animal

48

sacrifices were merely a shadow of the real thing to come. The real thing was Jesus and, whereas the old sacrifices only covered sins, the ultimate sacrifice of Jesus would actually take them away.

The old sacrifices left you with your guilty, defiled sin-consciousness. The blood of the Lamb of God, however, has the power to cleanse your conscience.

That's exactly what the writer of Hebrews goes on to explain:

Now where remission of these [sins] is, there is no more offering for sin. Having therefore, brethren, boldness to enter into the holiest by the blood of Jesus, By a new and living way, which he hath consecrated for us, through the veil, that is to say, his flesh; And having an high priest over the house of God; Let us draw near with a true heart in full assurance of faith, having our hearts sprinkled from an evil conscience, and our bodies washed with pure water. **(Hebrews 10:18-22)**

Notice that word "remission" in the above passage. It's the word that describes what the blood of Jesus does to our sins.

The old covenant sacrifices brought atonement (covering). The blood of Jesus brings remission (a complete taking away).

That's exactly what Jesus told His disciples His blood would do in Matthew 26:27-28:

And he took the cup, and gave thanks, and gave it to them, saying, Drink ye all of it; For this is my blood of the new testament, which is shed for many for the remission of sins.

When you made Jesus Lord of your life, God didn't just start ignoring your sins. He didn't just throw a blanket over them to keep them out of sight. He removed them. He took them away!

Renewing your mind to this fact is vital to operating in the fullness of the anointing.

I hear far too many believers whining and groveling before

God saying things such as, "I'm not worthy, Lord." Or, "I'm just an old filthy sinner."

That's wallowing in sin-consciousness and it's totally counter to the flow of the anointing.

When you have been purged by the blood of Jesus, you no longer carry the guilt of sin. The key is to renew your mind to the reality that is already present.

Meditate on the following verse until it sinks deeply into your heart and mind:

For he hath made him to be sin for us, who knew no sin; that we might be made the righteousness of God in him. **(2 Corinthians 5:21)**

No matter what you've done in the past. No matter what you may have participated in, the blood is stronger.

If you are in the Anointed One and His anointing, then you have been justified, reconciled, and your sins have been taken away.

A clear understanding of that glorious truth is a vital key to flowing and living in the burden-removing, yoke-destroying power of God.

CHAPTER 9

THE ANOINTING OF KNOWLEDGE

And the spirit of the LORD shall rest upon him,...the spirit of knowledge and of the fear of the LORD. **(Isaiah 11:2)**

By this time you've become familiar with the key passage of scripture which anchors our understanding of the anointing. I'm talking, of course, about Isaiah 10:27:

And it shall come to pass in that day, that his burden shall be taken away from off thy shoulder, and his yoke from off thy neck, and the yoke shall be destroyed because of the anointing.

We haven't, up to this point however, talked about the interesting pair of verses that are found at the beginning of the very next chapter in Isaiah. It's a prophecy about Jesus being the "rod out of the stem of Jesse." Jesse, of course, was King David's father and Jesus descended from David.

These verses tell us a lot about the anointing that rested upon Jesus, and therefore resides within us:

And there shall come forth a rod out of the stem of Jesse, and a Branch shall grow out of his roots: And the spirit of the LORD shall rest upon him, the spirit of wisdom and understanding, the spirit of counsel and might, the spirit of knowledge and of the fear of the LORD; **(Isaiah 11:1-2)**

This remarkable passage of scripture shows that there are a number of different facets to the anointing.

The anointing that rested upon Jesus and flows through us today manifests in different ways depending upon the type of burden that needs to be removed or the type of yoke that needs to be destroyed.

There are types of yokes and burdens that can only be dealt with by the anointing of wisdom. Others require the anointing of understanding. There are times when nothing but the anointing of counsel will do. The point is, the anointing is like a Swiss Army knife with a blade for every occasion and every need.

For the purpose of this chapter, I want to focus on one particular aspect of the anointing. I want you to see some things regarding "the anointing of knowledge."

Two Kinds of Knowledge

There is a difference between the kind of knowledge that comes from God and knowledge you obtain through natural means; such as, reading or education.

When the Word talks about a "spirit of knowledge" in Isaiah 11:2, it is not talking about naturally acquired knowledge. It's talking about *supernaturally* acquired knowledge. This is knowledge you can't get unless God imparts it to you by the anointing of His Spirit.

We see how important this kind of revealed knowledge is to our lives in Proverbs 29:18:

Where there is no vision, the people perish: **(Proverbs 29:18)**

In Hebrew the word "vision" in this verse literally means "revelation" or "divinely revealed knowledge." In other words, without revelation knowledge from God, you're going to perish in the area of your life in which you lack knowledge.

Child of God, if you don't get into a position in which God can reveal some things to you, you're going to find yourself perishing in some areas of your life.

If you're perishing in your finances, it's probably because you lack some important knowledge in that area. If you're perishing where your health is concerned, there is something you need to know that you're presently ignorant about.

The prophet Hosea tells us the same thing:

My people are destroyed for lack of knowledge: **(Hosea 4:6)**

Do you know how the wisest man who ever lived (other than Jesus of Nazereth Himself) got his wisdom?

Look at the account of Solomon in 1 Kings, chapter three. There, we find the new, young king confessing to God that he didn't have a clue as to how to reign in the place of his father, David:

And now, O LORD my God, thou hast made thy servant king instead of David my father: and I am but a little child: I know not how to go out or come in. And thy servant is in the midst of thy people which thou hast chosen, a great people, that cannot be numbered nor counted for multitude. **(1 Kings 3:7-8)**

Solomon was literally saying, "Lord, I don't know the first thing about being a king." So, what did he do that made him world famous for his wisdom? We find out in the next verse:

Give therefore thy servant an understanding heart to judge thy people, that I may discern between good and bad: for who is able to judge this thy so great a people? And the speech pleased the Lord, that Solomon had asked this thing. **(1 Kings 3:9-10)**

In the Hebrew language, Solomon was literally asking God for a "hearing" heart.

Solomon was smart enough to know that if he was going to make it as a king, he needed knowledge from God, but he couldn't receive that knowledge unless he had the "ears" of his heart unplugged.

To put it in radio terms, he knew God was transmitting, but he needed his receiver tuned to God's frequency!

The term *heart,* in the Bible is synonomous with *spirit.* The heart of a man is the very center of his being. Solomon was saying, "Lord, give me a spirit that can hear from you."

Solomon's request pleased the Lord. In response, God sent Solomon an anointing of knowledge and, as a result, the fame of his wisdom, understanding and discernment circulated around the world.

The Anointing of Revealed Knowledge

When that aspect of the anointing called the "spirit of knowledge" hits you, burdens are going to be removed and yokes are going to be destroyed. Why? Because that's what anointings do!

Too many of God's people are burdened by ignorance. They need the anointing of knowledge to remove that burden.

"Well, Pastor Dollar, Solomon was in the Old Testament. How do I know that still applies in the New Testament?"

That's a good question. Let's answer it by going to the first chapter of Ephesians:

[I, Paul,] Cease not to give thanks for you, making mention of you in my prayers; That the God of our Lord Jesus Christ, the Father of glory, may give unto you <u>the spirit of wisdom and revelation</u> in the knowledge of him: The eyes of your understanding being enlightened... (Ephesians 1:16-18a)

Here, Paul calls the spirit of revealed knowledge "the spirit of wisdom and revelation." We still have it under the New Covenant because we still have burdens and yokes that only it can remove and destroy.

Now, by the mouths of two or more witnesses let a thing be established, so, look also at Colossians 1:9:

For this cause we also, since the day we heard it, do not cease to pray for you, and to desire <u>that ye might be filled with the knowledge of his will in all wisdom and spiritual understanding;</u> (Colossians 1:9)

There's that anointing for supernatural knowledge again. In this case, revealed knowledge of God's will.

This kind of knowledge is not fuzzy or partial. It is precise and complete.

When you get revealed knowledge about the will of God, you get a complete and accurate picture of what that will is.

The reason many people don't receive their healing is that they don't have revealed knowledge of God's will concerning their healing.

You ask them if it's God's will to heal them and they'll say things like, "I hope so." Or, "I think so." Mere head knowledge and study won't give you the confidence to get healed. You need revealed knowledge. Once the anointing of knowledge concerning God's will to heal you, hits you, brother, you will know without a doubt that God wants you healed.

Then, you're just a short step of faith away from seeing that healing manifest. The anointing of knowledge removes burdens and destroys yokes brought on by ignorance or uncertainty about the will of God.

The Rock of Revealed Knowledge

You may have heard at one time or another that the Apostle Peter was the "rock" on which Jesus said He would build the church. That's taught a lot in religious circles. Entire denominations have been founded on that belief. But there's just one problem. It's not true. The Bible doesn't teach that.

Look with me at the passage in question.

When Jesus came into the coasts of Caesarea Philippi, he asked his disciples, saying, Whom do men say that I the Son of man am? And they said, Some say that thou art John the Baptist: some, Elias; and others, Jeremias, or one of the prophets. He saith unto them, But whom say ye that I am? And Simon Peter answered and said, Thou art the Christ, the Son of the living God. And Jesus answered and said unto him, Blessed art thou, Simon Barjona: for flesh and blood hath not revealed it unto thee, but my Father which is in heaven. And I say also unto thee, That thou art Peter, and upon this rock I will build my church; and the gates of hell shall not prevail against it. (Matthew 16:13-18)

Now, when you read that it certainly sounds like Jesus was saying that Peter was the rock on which the Church would be built. But when you read it in the original Greek, it takes on an entirely different meaning.

You see, Jesus used two different Greek words for rock in that last sentence.

When He said, "Thou are *Peter*," Jesus used the word *petros* which is a Greek word for a little stone. When Jesus then said, "and upon this *rock* I will build my church...., He used a different word. He used the Greek word *petra* which means a massive foundational boulder-stone.

An accurate paraphrase from the Greek would read, "Peter, flesh and blood didn't just reveal to you that I am the Anointed One, God revealed it to you supernaturally by the Spirit. Now you are a little stone, but upon the massive rock of revelation knowledge I'm going to build my church and the gates of hell will not prevail against it."

Do you see it? Peter isn't the rock. *Revealed knowledge* is! That anointing of knowledge that we've been studying is the foundation upon which the entire body of Christ is built. It's that important.

CHAPTER 10

THE ANOINTING OF THE FEAR OF THE LORD

Blessed is every one that feareth the LORD; that walketh in his ways. (Psalm 128:1)

In the previous chapter, we saw that one of the aspects or ingredients of the anointing listed in Isaiah 11:2 was "the spirit of knowledge." In this chapter I want to highlight another item on that list that factors into the anointing to live victoriously. I'm talking about "the anointing of the fear of the Lord."

Let's see it in that passage of scripture once more:

And the spirit of the LORD shall rest upon him, the spirit of wisdom and understanding, the spirit of counsel and might, the spirit of knowledge <u>and of the fear of the LORD</u>. (Isaiah 11:2)

According to this passage there is a facet to the precious jewel called the anointing that can be identified as "the anointing of the fear of the Lord."

Unfortunately, the term "the fear of the Lord" is one of the most misunderstood in all of scripture.

When the Bible talks about the fear of the Lord, it's not referring to terror or anxiety. It's not the kind of fear instilled by concern for your safety or dread of some terrible thing happening.

No, this kind of fear is a reverential, awesome respect. We'll get a clearer picture of what the fear of the Lord truly is by examining some of the scriptures that talk about it. Then we'll be able to find out what the <u>anointing of the fear of the Lord</u> is, and find out what kind of burdens it removes and yokes it destroys.

We find some interesting insights into the fear of the Lord in the 128th chapter of Psalms. Take a look at the first verse:

Blessed is every one that feareth the LORD; that walketh in his ways. **(Psalm 128:1)**

Now the word blessed literally means, "empowered to prosper." So, a valid translation of that verse would be, "Empowered to prosper is everyone who walks in the fear of the Lord."

If you can get the anointing of the fear of the Lord operating in your life, you're going to be empowered to prosper-empowered to be in control of your circumstances.

This verse also tells us that the fear of the Lord is synonymous with "walking in His ways." You can't operate in the fear of the Lord if you don't walk in His ways. How do you learn God's ways? By meditating on His Word and spending time with Him!

Now read the next few verses of Psalm 128 and we'll discover some more benefits of walking in the fear of the Lord:

For thou shalt eat the labour of thine hands: happy shalt thou be, and it shall be well with thee. Thy wife shall be as a fruitful vine by the sides of thine house: thy children like olive plants round about thy table. Behold, that thus shall the man be blessed that feareth the LORD. **(Psalms 128:2-4)**

Making the choice to operate in the fear of the Lord will have a powerful, positive impact on your home, your family and your quality of life.

Does that make you want to know more about living in the fear of the Lord? It does for me. Let's look at another verse of scripture for more insight.

The fear of the LORD is to hate evil: pride, and arrogancy, and the evil way, and the froward mouth, do I hate. **(Proverbs 8:13)**

Walking in the anointing of the fear of the Lord is more than just loving the things that God loves. It also involves hating the things that He hates.

Hate is a strong term, isn't it? It's a powerful emotion, but it's the only appropriate emotion to feel when you really see what sin and evil produces in the lives of people.

All the things this verse lists-evil, pride, arrogance, and "froward" or corrupt speech-bring destruction, heartache, misery and death to the objects of God's love and affection-people.

When you really get a revelation of what evil is and what it does to people, there is no other appropriate response but hatred.

God isn't against fornication and adultery because He's out to keep you from having fun. He's against it because it brings misery and death to whomever it touches. He *hates* sin because He *loves* you. And if you're going to walk in the fear of the Lord, you're going to have to hate it too.

That's really all the fear of the Lord is-identifying with and aligning yourself with the attitudes of God.

It is choosing an alliance with God's priorities instead of your own. It's choosing an alliance with God's ways instead of the world's. It's choosing an alliance with God's hatreds instead of your own lusts.

The fear of the Lord is a *holy alliance* rather than an unholy alliance.

The Benefits of the Fear of the Lord

Some people don't choose the fear of the Lord because they don't see any benefits in it. After all, they say, "At least sin contains some pleasure."

When I hear someone say something like that I know they are ignorant of two things. They're ignorant of the wages of sin (death), and they're ignorant of the benefits of walking in the fear of the Lord.

We've already looked at some of the benefits, but let's explore some more. Look at Psalm 34:7, for example:

The angel of the LORD encampeth round about them that fear him, and delivereth them. **(Psalm 34:7)**

How would you like to have mighty angels encamped around you ready to deliver you from all trouble? Well, it's a benefit of the fear of the Lord.

I've met hundreds of Christians who were desperately trying to figure out a way to get delivered from their negative circumstances. They would have climbed any mountain to get free and all the time they could have been experiencing angelic deliverance by choosing to operate in the spirit of the fear of the Lord.

It shouldn't surprise us that the anointing of the fear of the Lord brings deliverance. It's what anointings do-remove burdens and destroy yokes.

We find another benefit of this aspect of the anointing in the following verses:

O taste and see that the LORD is good: blessed is the man that trusteth in him. O fear the LORD, ye his saints: for there is no want to them that fear him. (Psalm 34:8-9)

Would you consider the ability to live free from want, lack and insufficiency a significant benefit? Of course you would! And according to this passage that's exactly what comes from operating in the fear of the Lord.

We see a similar promise in Proverbs 19:23:

The fear of the LORD leads to life, So that one may sleep satisfied, untouched by evil. (Proverbs 19:23 NASB)

What a powerful, threefold promise this is! Life, rest, and being untouchable by evil are all benefits of the fear of the Lord.

Recent studies have shown that Americans are more fearful and anxious than at any time in our history. We're a nation filled with people afraid of being touched by evil. But if you have the anointing of the fear of the Lord working for you, you sleep like a baby knowing all your needs are met and no evil can touch you.

Giving and the Fear of the Lord

There is an element to walking in the fear of the Lord that most of us have overlooked. We don't usually associate *giving* with the fear of the Lord, but the Bible does. Look at Acts, chapter ten:

Now there was a certain man at Caesarea named Cornelius, a centurion of what was called the Italian cohort, a devout man, and <u>one who feared God with all his household, and gave many alms to the Jewish people</u>, and prayed to God continually. (Acts 10:1-2 NASB)

Here, we see having a holy fear of God linked to the giving of alms or money. Being that kind of person put Cornelius in a position to receive an angelic visitation and a special touch from God.

About the ninth hour of the day he clearly saw in a vision an angel of God who had just come in to him, and said to him, "Cornelius!" And fixing his gaze upon him and being much alarmed, he said, "What is it, Lord?" And he said to him, "<u>Your prayers and alms have ascended as a memorial before God</u>. (Acts 10:3-4 NASB)

Did you catch that? Not only did Cornelius' prayers ascend to heaven, so did his giving! The man's generosity got God's attention and put him in position to receive a miracle.

We see another great example of how the fear of the Lord is linked to giving in the life of Abraham. Look at this passage in Genesis, chapter 22, in which Abraham, out of obedience to God is about to sacrifice his miracle-child, Isaac:

And the angel of the LORD called unto him out of heaven, and said, Abraham, Abraham: and he said, Here am I. And he said, Lay not thine hand upon the lad, neither do thou any thing unto him: for <u>now I know that thou fearest God, seeing thou hast not withheld thy son, thine only son from me</u>. (Genesis 22:11-12)

How did this angel know that Abraham walked in the fear of the Lord? Because of his willingness to give God what He asked for.

A willingness to give God what belongs to Him is a major indicator of the fear of the Lord.

When I hear someone say they can't afford to tithe, I know immediately they won't enjoy the benefits of the anointing of the fear of the Lord. If they were walking in it, they would be giving God what belonged to Him and trusting Him to meet their needs. After all, we just read that those who fear the Lord are satisfied and have no want.

Obedience, especially in the realm of giving, is the clearest indicator that a person is walking in the fear of the Lord. You can't fear God and not obey Him.

Why do many believers fail to obey God? Because, in reality, they fear man more than they fear God. Jesus warned us about that in Matthew 10:28 when He said:

Fear not them which kill the body, but are not able to kill the soul: but rather fear him which is able to destroy both soul and body in hell.

Fear of man will keep you from sharing your faith because you don't want anyone to make fun of you. Fear of man will keep you from standing up against peer pressure and risking being thought of as strange or uncool.

If you're in bondage to the fear of man, that fear will always be pulling you away from obedience to God. Throughout scripture we see the fear of the Lord being linked to obeying God. Another great example is in Ecclesiastes 12:13:

Let us hear the conclusion of the whole matter: Fear God, and keep his commandments: for this is the whole duty of man.

There it is. "Fear God, and keep His commandments." The two go hand in hand. And you'll never move into the fear of God until you make a quality decision not to be in fear of man.

In these last days, it is vital that we begin to cultivate the fear of the Lord. The good news is, it's an ingredient of the Anointed One and His anointing. The anointing of the fear of the Lord is available right now to destroy yokes and remove burdens, as only it can.

CHAPTER 11

THE ANOINTING OF THE SPIRIT OF THE LORD

The Spirit of the Lord is upon me, because he hath anointed me... **(Luke 4:18)**

To truly understand how the anointing empowers us to live, you must first understand how it operated in the Anointed One, Jesus.

To get that information we must go back to the time when Jesus first became anointed. We see a description of that precise moment in Luke, chapter three:

Now when all the people were baptized, it came to pass, that Jesus also being baptized, and praying, the heaven was opened, And <u>the Holy Ghost descended in a bodily shape like a dove upon him,</u> and a voice came from heaven, which said, Thou art my beloved Son; in thee I am well pleased. **(Luke 3:21-22)**

It comes as a shock to some people to discover that Jesus wasn't always anointed. They have a religious concept of Him crawling around as a little baby doing miracles and being aware that He's the Son of God. That's not what the Bible teaches.

Yes, Jesus was the Son of God from the moment He was born, but He was not *operating* as God. He was operating as a man, with all the limitations of human flesh.

That was the case until that day on the banks of the Jordan River when the Holy Ghost descended on Jesus and anointed Him.

There is no record of Jesus ever performing a miracle before that day. We don't see Him removing any burdens or destroying any yokes.

In fact, there is not one indication that Jesus did anything out of the ordinary prior to being anointed with the Spirit. But once He was anointed, He began to prophesy, preach, work miracles and do everything He saw the Father doing.

Look at what the Word says happened immediately after that baptism:

And Jesus being full of the Holy Ghost returned from Jordan, and was led by the Spirit into the wilderness. **(Luke 4:1)**

Now that Jesus is anointed we see that He's filled with the Holy Spirit and is now being led by that Spirit.

After spending 40 days in the wilderness, we next find Jesus walking into His old hometown and making an earth-shaking pronouncement. It was a pronouncement in which He declared to His Jewish listeners that He was the Anointed One prophesied by the prophet Isaiah:

And he came to Nazareth, where he had been brought up: and, as his custom was, he went into the synagogue on the sabbath day, and stood up for to read. And there was delivered unto him the book of the prophet Esaias. And when he had opened the book, he found the place where it was written,The Spirit of the Lord is upon me, because he hath anointed me to preach the gospel to the poor; he hath sent me to heal the brokenhearted, to preach deliverance to the captives, and recovering of sight to the blind, to set at liberty them that are bruised, To preach the acceptable year of the Lord. And he closed the book, and he gave it again to the minister, and sat down. And the eyes of all them that were in the synagogue were fastened on him. And he began to say unto them, This day is this scripture fulfilled in your ears. **(Luke 4:16-21)**

I want you to take special notice of the first words Jesus quoted from Isaiah. He said, "The Spirit of the Lord is upon me, because he hath anointed me..."

Now compare that to what we've seen from Isaiah, chapter 11:

And there shall come forth a rod out of the stem of Jesse, and a Branch shall grow out of his roots: And the spirit of the LORD shall rest upon him... **(Isaiah 11:1-2)**

This is talking about the anointing of the Spirit of the Lord.

To *anoint* literally means "to rub, paint or smear a substance on a person. When Jesus was anointed with the Spirit of the Lord, the power and essence of God Himself was painted on Him.

When you receive the anointing, something, or rather someone is being painted onto your natural flesh adding God's *super* to your *natural.* Who is that someone? The Holy Ghost!

Jesus talks about the ministry of the Holy Ghost in John 14:26:

But the Comforter, which is the Holy Ghost, whom the Father will send in my name, he shall teach you all things, and bring all things to your remembrance, whatsoever I have said unto you.

This and many other scriptures about the Holy Ghost make one thing clear. The Spirit of God is not an *it.* The Spirit is a *person,* and therefore has a personality.

What are the characteristics of that personality? One major one is mentioned in the scripture we just read. He is a *comforter.*

It is very much in keeping with the Spirit's personality to bring comfort.

Another characteristic of the Spirit's personality is that whenever He shows up, miracles happen. We see this aspect of His personality in this familiar verse:

How God anointed Jesus of Nazareth with the Holy Ghost and with power: who went about doing good, and healing all that were oppressed of the devil; **(Acts 10:38)**

Notice the key words there. God *anointed* Jesus with *the Holy Ghost.* And what was the result? Miracles. Burdens removed. Yokes destroyed.

A personality determines how someone acts. Well, this is how the Holy Spirit acts. He anoints. He comforts. He heals. He does good. He brings burden-removing, yoke-destroying power on the scene. That's just how He is.

When we see Jesus in the New Testament-the miracle-working person of power, knowledge and wisdom-we're not seeing someone acting as God on the earth. We're seeing what a man can do when He's anointed by the Spirit without measure. (John 3:34)

If Jesus was accessing His power as God the Son when He healed the sick and cast out devils, we're in trouble, because He said greater works than I do shall *you* do. (John 14:12) And we're not God!

But if He was operating as a Holy Ghost-filled man when He did those things, then we have some hope, because we have access to the anointing of the Holy Ghost too.

The fact is, Jesus explicitly tells us that the anointing of the Holy Ghost is our source of power. He did so in Acts, chapter one, right before He ascended to the Father:

But ye shall receive power, after that the Holy Ghost is come upon you: and ye shall be witnesses unto me both in Jerusalem, and in all Judaea, and in Samaria, and unto the uttermost part of the earth. (Acts 1:8)

When the anointing of the Holy Ghost comes upon you, you receive "power" -burden-removing and yoke-destroying.

CHAPTER 12

KEYS TO LIVING IN THE ANOINTING

I am crucified with Christ: nevertheless I live; yet not I, but Christ liveth in me: and the life which I now live in the flesh I live by the faith of the Son of God, who loved me, and gave himself for me. **(Galatians 2:20)**

It's one thing to know what the anointing is. And it's certainly important to know Who *brings* the anointing. But you're not all the way there unless you know practical ways to *live* in that anointing. That's what this chapter is all about.

As we look through the Bible, we can look at times in which people accessed the anointing and we can identify keys to flowing in it and cooperating with it. We see one of those times in Acts, chapter three where Peter and John were heading for the Temple at the Gate Beautiful:

Now Peter and John went up together into the temple at the hour of prayer, being the ninth hour. And a certain man lame from his mother's womb was carried, whom they laid daily at the gate of the temple which is called Beautiful, to ask alms of them that entered into the temple; Who seeing Peter and John about to go into the temple asked an alms. And Peter, fastening his eyes upon him with John, said, Look on us. **(Acts 3:1-4)**

We have here a man with a terrible yoke of bondage. He had been crippled since birth and, as a result, had to eke out an existence as a beggar.

When he asked Peter and John for a little money, he didn't know he was talking to anointed men.

Now, Peter knew that if this man was going to receive any-thing through the anointing, one thing was going to have to change. The man was going to have to get *expectant.*

At that moment the man didn't expect anything except some loose change. But Peter and John knew that if they could get him to take his attention off of his problem and get expec-tant about having his burden removed he would get healed. That's why John said, "Look on us."

You can't get a miracle from God if your focus is on your problem. That's where so many Christians miss it. They're so focused on their need that they never look up at the source of their answer.

Now notice how the man responded:

And he gave heed unto them, <u>expecting</u> to receive some-thing of them. (Acts 3:5)

What does it mean to give "heed" to something? It means to give highly focused attention with expectancy. With that in mind let me ask you a question. When you read the Bible, do you give it heed? In other words, do you give it focused atten-tion with expectancy?

Too many Christians open their Bibles expecting nothing. They read "by His stripes you were healed," and expect noth-ing. They read, "God takes pleasure in the prosperity of His servants," and expect nothing.

Listen to me, child of God, a major key to drawing on the anointing power of the Spirit is expectancy. Look at what it did for the beggar at the Gate Beautiful:

Then Peter said, Silver and gold have I none; but such as I have give I thee: In the name of Jesus Christ of Nazareth rise up and walk. And he took him by the right hand, and lifted him up: and immediately his feet and ankle bones received strength. And he leaping up stood, and walked, and entered with them into the temple, walking, and leaping, and praising God. (Acts 3:6-8)

The man's expectancy placed a demand on the anointing

that was in Peter. It drew the power of God out of him and destroyed his yoke.

Expectancy is a major key to living and flowing in the anointing.

Shaking Off the Unexpected

Not every yoke or burden that will try to attach itself to you in life can be seen coming from a mile away.

Sometimes trouble shows up suddenly and unexpectedly. But that doesn't mean the anointing won't do its work. There are, however, some keys to dealing with these kinds of attacks. We see one important key in Acts 28 where Paul is ministering to some people on an island near the place his ship had sank:

And when Paul had gathered a bundle of sticks, and laid them on the fire, there came a viper out of the heat, and fastened on his hand. And when the barbarians saw the venomous beast hang on his hand, they said among themselves, No doubt this man is a murderer, whom, though he hath escaped the sea, yet vengeance suffereth not to live. **(Acts 28:3-4)**

Paul is going along, minding his own business, trying to be helpful in building a fire, when suddenly a poisonous snake attaches itself to his hand.

The pagan natives of that island assumed Paul was being punished by the gods for some crime. But watch how Paul responded:

And he shook off the beast into the fire, and felt no harm. Howbeit they looked when he should have swollen, or fallen down dead suddenly: but after they had looked a great while, and saw no harm come to him, they changed their minds, and said that he was a god. **(Acts 28:5-6)**

The anointing that was on Paul protected Him from any harm. This, of course, is consistent with the kind of power Jesus said Holy Ghost-anointed believers would operate in:

And these signs shall follow them that believe; In my name shall they cast out devils; they shall speak with new tongues; They shall take up serpents; and if they drink any deadly thing, it shall not hurt them; they shall lay hands on the sick, and they shall recover. **(Mark 16:17-18)**

There is one thing Paul did that I want you to notice. We're told that when that snake latched onto his hand, he "shook off the beast into the fire."

When the devil came to try to damage him, *he shook it off.*

"What are you trying to say preacher?"

Just this. There will be times in your life in which the enemy is going to pop up and bite you. That bite will carry some potential poison that can bring death into your life unless you do as Paul did and *shake it off.*

That bite may come in the form of a brother or sister in Christ who hurts you deeply. You'll have an opportunity to receive the deadly poison of unforgiveness and bitterness if you let that hurt remain there hanging on you.

You must shake it off if the anointing is going to protect you and deliver you. You shake off that hurt by choosing to forgive as an act of your will.

When symptoms come and try to attach themselves to you, shake them off. When lack jumps up and bites you, shake it off.

The Anointed One and His anointing resides in you to deliver you from all harm and every attack, but it can't if you allow something to cling to you instead of shaking it off into the fire!

Make up your mind right now to cooperate and flow with the anointing by keeping your expectancy high and shaking off hurts and attacks when they come.

You're anointed and you have the ability to win even when things look impossible. You're not a mere natural man or woman. You're a born-again person filled and painted with the very power and personality of God, the Holy Spirit!

Lift your hands to heaven right now and make this confession:

Heavenly Father, in the name of Jesus I want to see Your power operating and flowing in my life as I see it flowing in the lives of those in the Bible. Give me a hunger and thirst for Your burden-removing, yoke-destroying power. In the name of Jesus, I'll walk in the anointing of the Anointed One. I'll get results today. I'll get results tomorrow. I'll get greater and greater results until Jesus returns because I am anointed!

CONCLUSION

But the anointing which ye have received of him abideth in you, and ye need not that any man teach you: but as the same anointing teacheth you of all things, and is truth, and is no lie, and even as it hath taught you, ye shall abide in him. **(1 John 2:27)**

It should be clear to you by now that the anointing is available to every believer. And it is an absolute necessity to have if you expect to live victoriously in these dark last days.

Jesus is not returning for a people staggering under crushing burdens and enslaved by yokes of bondage. He's returning for a people living in freedom. And the only thing that can bring that freedom is the burden-removing, yoke-destroying power of the anointing.

Nothing else will do. Nothing else is sufficient for the hour.

Now, in these closing pages I want to share some final thoughts from the Word that I believe will help you live in the anointing in a fuller way than you ever imagined.

Strength in the Anointing

We're living in days in which, if you're going to make it all the way, you're going to need supernatural strength.

Neither you nor I have enough strength in our own natural ability to live victoriously and consistently in these last days. The good news is, we have a inexhaustible supply of strength and power residing on the inside of us. That source is the anointing.

Look at the old, familiar scripture in Philippians 4:13, for a moment, and translate the word Christ into its original meaning:

I can do all things through [the Anointed One and His anointing] which strengtheneth me.

Do you see it? The anointing empowers you to do "all things." This verse is even more exciting when you read it in the Amplified Bible:

I have strength for all things in [the Anointed One and His anointing] Who empowers me [I am ready for anything and equal to anything through Him Who infuses inner strength into me]; I am self-sufficient in [the anointing's] sufficiency.

Don't look to some source outside yourself for strength. That source, the anointing, is in you.

Second Peter 1:3 tells us we've been given everything that pertains to life and godliness. Whatever you need to get to the finish line of life a winner is right there on the inside of you.

Don't you see, it's not enough to have the power in you. You must *know* that it's there in order for it to do you any good.

I can deposit a million dollars into your bank account, but you'll still be worrying about finances and living like a pauper if you don't know it's there. You must be aware of something in order to access it.

When you were born-again, God made a deposit in you that is worth far more than a million dollars. He put something in you that can get you healed, keep you safe, keep your marriage together, keep your children from going the way of the world, and prosper you in every way.

The anointing is that deposit. You are fully equipped.

Faith and the Anointing

It's one thing to know that a deposit has been made in your account. It's another thing to know how to make a withdrawal.

We find a key to accessing the great wealth and power of the anointing in Ephesians, chapter three:

That he would grant you, according to the riches of his glory, to be strengthened with might by his Spirit in the

inner man; That [the Anointed One and His anointing] may dwell in your hearts by faith. **(Ephesians 3:16-17)**

There's your withdrawal form-faith! The strength and might that is dwelling in you dwells there "by faith."

If you have no faith in the presence and power of the anointing, you're not going to have any expectancy of it. And as we've seen, expectancy is a major key to seeing that anointing flow and work to remove burdens and destroy yokes.

When trouble comes, you need to have rock-solid confidence that the anointing is there, and that it is more than enough to get you through. We must be anointing-inside minded.

That anointing is the power to look at a mountain of debt and know that the anointing-in-you is going to destroy that yoke of indebtedness.

Not only do you have Heaven as your ultimate home, you have some Heaven on the inside of you now, in this life.

The Final Result of the Anointing

We just learned from Ephesians 3:17 that the anointing dwells in our hearts by faith. Now, in closing, I want you to look at the next few verses and see where all this ends up:

That [the Anointed One and His anointing] may dwell in your hearts by faith; that ye, being rooted and grounded in love, May be able to comprehend with all saints what is the breadth, and length, and depth, and height; And to know the love of [the Anointed One and His anointing], which passeth knowledge, that ye might be filled with all the fulness of God. **(Ephesians 3:17-19)**

There it is. We have the anointing working by faith so we can ultimately comprehend the love of the Anointed One and His anointing! When that happens we get "filled with all the fullness of God."

What a thought. To be filled with God Himself with a complete comprehension and understanding of His love for us. And that is something that only the anointing can do.

The reason we've been given the anointing is that it equips us and enables us to get all the way home-all the way to our final destination.

Is that destination Heaven? Yes, but it's more than that. God's plan for you is much more than just making it to Heaven by the skin of your teeth.

Your destiny is to get there in victory-fully conformed to the image of the Anointed One, experiencing freedom from all yokes and burdens, exercising dominion over your enemy, being filled with all the fullness of God.

Decide right now to yield to the flow of that power and presence called the anointing. Make a quality decision to avoid all antichrists. Break all unholy alliances. Then get ready to experience the value and blessing of the anointing.

Get ready to experience sweet fellowship with the Anointed One, Jesus.